MW01289760

A Concise Guide to Companion Planting

by Tobias Moore

Copyright © 2019 Tobias Moore
All rights reserved.
ISBN: 9781073001088

CONTENTS

I	History	1
II	What it is	3
III	Benefits	5
IV	Soil	7
V	Unwanted Guests	13
VI	Wanted Guests	37
VII	Plants	45
VIII	Reference Tables	67
IX	References	79
	About the Author	83

Cucumbers, tomatoes, carrots, & marigold

GIVING THANKS

Earth, Sun, Water, Air.

Calendula, carrots, herbs, & broccoli

I
HISTORY

Companion planting has been around for thousands of years. As far back as 3000 BCE the Sumerians and Egyptians planted trees to protect their crops from the hot summer sun.

In ancient Indian writings there are many references to companion planting such as avoiding certain plant combinations and growing and turning plants into the soil like sesame as a means to improve soil structure and harvest outcomes.

Some eastern tribes of North America grew three plants together, known as the Three Sisters (corn, beans, and squash), because of beneficial effects they had on each other. Corn gave the beans something to climb, squash suppressed weeds, helped with water retention and pest control, while the beans enriched and added nitrogen to the soil.

The Chinese grew mosquito ferns near rice crops to help fix nitrogen and to block sunlight from competing plants.

As far back as the 3rd century BCE Theophrastus, in his *De Causis Plantarum*, talked about sweet bay and cabbage being antagonistic to the grapevine (Book II, Section 18.4) while a fig tree planted near squills will help it grow faster and not be plagued by worms (Book III, Section 13).

During the Renaissance the French started potager gardens, or kitchen gardens, where multiple vegetables and flowers were grown together as a means of optimizing food production and increasing the overall beauty of the garden.

Stepping into the 20th century Richard B. Gregg in

1943 published a pamphlet called *Companion and Protective Plants* that summarized Dr. Ehrenfried E. Pfeiffer's and Dr. Eric Sabarth's research on companion planting.

The permaculture movement, which arose in the 70's, utilized companion planting to create permanent cultured gardens that mimic nature.

II
WHAT IT IS

In a nutshell companion planting is growing multiple things together in order to gain some benefit (more on benefits in next chapter). Some things grown together in companion planting are vegetables, fruits, flowers, mushrooms, mosses, grasses, ferns, trees, shrubs, and bushes.

Some factors to consider when companion planting:

- Light needs (sun with shade loving plants)
- Deep with shallow rooted plants
- Slow with fast growing plants
- Nutritional needs (heavy vs light feeders)
- Water needs
- Soil condition
- Soil pH
- Environment (rocky, sandy, grassy, clay, dry, wet, and so forth)
- Colors (hues, tints, tones, shades, and intensity)
- Size
- High versus low maintenance
- Upright with sprawling plants
- Forms (shape and size)
- Layout (structured, chaotic, layered, leveled, wavy, linear, vertical, circular, etc.)
- Contrasts
- Smells
- Textures

- Themes (love, airy, mysterious, beauty, meditative, invigorating, dyes, and so on)
- Bloom times (early with late)
- Genetic similarities (tomatoes, peppers, and potatoes for example)
- Insect attraction or repelling
- Energetics (how it makes you feel, think, remember, et cetera)
- Spiritual
- Medicinal

Ways of companion planting:
- Border planting
- Orderly intercropping
- Scattered intercropping
- Accents
- Size levels
- Hanging (nasturtiums in greenhouse for instance)
- Potting (mints and other invasive plants)
- Climbing (cucumbers, peas, etc.)
- Creeping (nasturtiums, purslane, some thymes)
- Mulching with aromatics (might not want to plant invasive mints in garden beds but they can be planted in proximity and then cut and used as mulch around other plants)

When it comes to choosing plants start with what you want. Once you know what you want and where you're going to grow it, the next thing to do is figure out what plants are beneficial and which are not (refer to plant profiles starting on page 45).

III
BENEFITS

There are likely hundreds of different benefits to companion planting. In my research and experience I have found the following to be the most important:

- Inviting beneficial insects such as pollinators, parasitoids, and predators
- Deterring and repelling pests
- Deterring diseases
- Supporting other plants
- Aesthetic properties
- Trapping unwanted insects
- Sheltering
- Supplying nutrients
- Nutritional mulch
- Wind blocks and creating shade
- Optimizing space usage
- Catch crops
- Suppressing weeds
- Improving flavor
- Strengthening and increasing growth rates
- Improving soil and fixing nitrogen
- Minimizing erosion
- Creating diversity and microclimates
- Improving yields

Spinach, orache, borage, & seed arugula

IV
SOIL

I believe all garden books should give a little attention to the soil. For healthy soil = healthy plants. By just giving the soil some attention we can avoid many of the problems companion planting seeks to address. The healthier a plant is the less likely it will get sick, be attacked, or fail to thrive.

Many great books have been written on soil composition, structure, pH, drainage, organisms, nutrients, microbes, textures, consistency, and so on. This is not one of them. For a concise guide on soil building see my upcoming book, *A Concise Guide to Building Healthy Soil.*

Three important soil factors to consider:
- pH (potential of Hydrogen)
- Nutritional content (macro and micro)
- Drainage

When it comes to pH most vegetables like neutral soil (6.6-7.3). Even so, some plants like more acidic soils such as azaleas, rhododendrons, cranberries, and blueberries, while others prefer more alkaline soils such as barberries, black currents, and asparagus. See page 69-70 for pH preferences.

Most garden stores sell test strips or gadgets that can measure soil pH.

Organic means of lowering (acidifying) soil pH (ordered from subtle to most intense)
- Compost

- Manure
- Alfalfa meal
- Used coffee grounds
- Leaf compost
- Pine needles
- Peat moss (not sustainable)
- Elemental sulfur

Organic means of raising pH (ordered from subtle to most intense)

- Oyster shell lime
- Limestone
- Wood ash (hardwood)

Imagine surviving on saltines only: not possible. In the same way plants need nutrition to grow and thrive.

With carbon, hydrogen, and oxygen, plants also need macronutrients such as nitrogen, phosphorus, potassium, calcium, magnesium, and sulfur to flourish.

In addition to these macronutrients plants also need micronutrients such as iron, boron, copper, chlorine, manganese, molybdenum, zinc, cobalt, aluminum, silicon, selenium, sodium, and nickel.

When it comes to plant nutrition most garden books focus on the big three: nitrogen, phosphorus, and potassium. Nitrogen is essential for plant growth and reproduction. It is a key component of chlorophyll, an essential ingredient of photosynthesis. Nitrogen is also a major component of amino acids, which play a large part in giving a plant structure and helping with the biochemical reactions necessary for life. Phosphorus is important for root development, plant maturity, fruit and seed production, photosynthesis, cell respiration, energy storage, energy transfer, cell division, cell growth, stem integrity, and disease resistance. Potassium is essential for a plant's overall health, its ability to deal with weather and temperatures, photosynthesis, protein synthesis, and a plant's immunity to diseases and predation.

Addressing nutrient deficiencies

Nutrient	Supplement
Nitrogen	Alfalfa and blood meal, fish emulsion, guano, soybean meal
Phosphorus	Bonemeal and rock of phosphate
Potassium	Granite meal, wood ash and greensand
Magnesium	Epsom salts, dolomitic lime
Calcium	Gypsum, calcitic lime, oyster shells, crushed chicken egg shells
Sulfur	Flowers of sulfur and gypsum
Boron	Borax
Other micronutrients	Kelp meal and seaweed

Here's a basic rundown of how I build good soil. It does not matter what soil you have, just feed it good stuff and you will eventually have good soil. Here follows my dos and don'ts.

Don'ts

- Excessive tilling, especially on windy days because you will lose some coveted top soil as well as ruin soil structure and kill off organisms. If you till don't do it when the soil is really wet or extremely dry.
- Pesticides, herbicides, or other toxins
- Synthetic fertilizers
- Walking on beds and compacting them
- Changing pH quickly
- Empty beds (leads to erosion, compaction, and unwanted plants)
- Always growing the same vegetables in the same beds
- Monocultures (growing just one kind of plant in beds)
- Intensely watering or under watering

Do's

- Green manures / cover crops
- Mulching
- Adding compost, vermicompost, and manure
- Teas (compost, manure, plants like comfrey and nettles)
- Adding leaf mold. A simple way to make leaf mold is to make at least a three foot diameter cylinder with fencing that's four feet high and fill it with a bunch of leaves. Let it be for a year or so.
- Raised beds that are never walked on
- Crop rotation
- Water gently

- Fall sheet mulching (adding a few inches of brown to green materials and throwing in some worms to work through the winter)
- Weed out unwelcome plants
- Tilling with chickens
- Polyculture (growing more than one plant in garden bed: biodiversity)
- Mining with deep rooting plants
- Adding amendments
    - Kelp meal
    - Greensand
    - Bone and blood meals
    - Rock phosphate
    - Shellfish meal
    - Dried, powdered egg shells
    - Rock dusts (glacial, basalt, azomite)

Lettuce, herbs, & onions

IV
UNWANTED GUESTS

While I have nothing against slugs, deer, or any other critter, I'm definitely not wanting them to eat my fruits and veggies. Companion planting offers many strategies for dealing with unwanted guests in the garden.

Some Plant Strategies to deal with predation
- Hairy, waxy, or tough leaves
- Thorns
- Bitter and toxic compounds
- Masking smells and colors
- Obstructing views (hedges for deer and hiding colors from some insects with plant variations)
- Intensity of aromas
- Inviting beneficial insects to eat unwanted guests
- Decoys
- Trapping

General things that can be done to help deter unwanted guests:
- *Fencing and Barriers*
  - Around garden
  - Around individual plants and trees
  - Burying chicken wire to prevent burrowing animals from entering
  - Row covers
  - Greenhouses

- Netting to prevent birds from eating fruits
- Collars around tree trunks and plant stems to prevent animals or insects from climbing trees or getting at plants
- Electric fencing
- Mulching and plastic coverings
- Spreading coffee grounds, clays, diatomaceous earth, and other organic materials to either kill or deter pests.

- *Cleaning up, maintenance, and other things*
  - No brush piles for hiding animals
  - Avoid leaving things that would invite trouble like foods
  - Not putting meats, bones, cheeses, or oils in compost that attracts rodents and other critters
  - Cleaning up weedy areas
  - Cleaning up any garbage and keeping trashcan lids tightly shut
  - Cleaning up around bird feeders and making them inaccessible to squirrels
  - Fixing fences and other things around the garden
  - Improving soil health
  - Planting resistant plants
  - Plant timing and placements (planting earlier or after an insect comes around will help avoid problems)
  - Crop rotations
  - Companion planting
  - Soil solarization (wet soil, lay transparent plastic on bed, and allow

the sun to cook the soil for a couple of months)

- o Adding compost
- o Light tilling
- o Adding specific herbal teas
- o Handpicking

- *Deterrents*
  - o *Scents*: garlic, castor oil, predator urine, specific plants and flowers
  - o *Sights*: shiny metal foils and reflective tapes and mulches, motion sensor lights, hedges, sheets or some other opaque material to block sight, faux predators, scare crows, dogs and cats to chase away or kill unwanted garden guests
  - o *Sounds*: noise makers, screaming and yelling to scare away animals, popping off a round
  - o *Physical*: motion sensor sprinklers, hosing cats and dogs to train them to stay out of garden beds (good luck on that one), barriers, copper stripping, mulches, collars, floating row covers
  - o *Tastes*: spraying plants with garlic and hot pepper teas
- *Traps*: lights, pheromones, sticky traps, trap crops, liquid traps (example: beer for slugs)
- *Killing*: guns, bows, squashing, swatting, zapping, and buckets of soapy water to drop live bugs in.

Unwanted Animals

Name	Damage	Solutions
Bear	Stepping on beds, breaking down fences, eating berries.	Heavy fencing, avoid leaving out food, electric wire, animal relocation, noise deterrents (shooting guns, bull horns), and dogs.
Birds	They eat fruits, grains, seeds, and welcomed guests. They also dig in the beds. Generally they are more beneficial than not.	Scarecrows, shiny tapes, sound makers, netting over fruits, faux predators, cats.
Chipmunks	They uproot bulbs, eat nuts and seeds.	Traps, spraying plants with liquefied garlic/hot pepper puree, predator urine, chicken wire, clear out debris, owls, cats, and castor plant.

Deer	They totally eat your garden up as well as step all over your beds ☹ I had one break into a greenhouse and top some tomatoes.	An eight foot fence, predator urine, dogs, surrounding plants with deer resistant plants (thistles, foxglove), hedges, scaring them, spraying plants with unpleasant tastes.
Dogs and cats	They'll dig and poop in your garden, step on plants and knock things over.	Fences, spray with water, painstakingly and patiently training them, mesh wire or mulch in newly seeded beds to deter digging, mulching with pennyroyal, rue, and other strong smelling plants.
Gophers	They will eat roots and then pull the plants underground to finish them off. They will also feed on	Put raw fish scraps, castor oil, coffee grounds, or other smelly things into their holes.

	tree bark and chew irrigation lines.	Grow gopher spurge, castor beans, alliums, mints, daffodils, sage, marigolds, and lavender to lessen gopher presence. Invite barn owls with nesting boxes, snakes with rock piles, and let your cats do what they do underground fencing, box traps
Moles	They will eat worms, insects, and sometimes bulbs and roots. Most of the damage comes from dislodging plants as they burrow.	What works for gophers above will generally work for moles. In addition try placing human hair into the holes. It's been said this helps deter moles. Trapping, inviting predators, and when you see

		the ground rising from the mole digging you can stomp hard on the burrow or use a shovel to kill the mole.
Rabbits	They eat a lot of different plants: greens, legumes, trees, brassica, herbs, berries, and ornamentals. They damage irrigation lines and can harm young trees.	Fencing is generally the best option, though rabbits will burrow underneath so you will have to bury fence a foot deep. Trapping. Getting rid of habitat such as brush piles and wild grass areas around garden. Dogs are useful to chase them off. Killing and eating.
Raccoons	They eat corn, berries, fruits, and a lot of vegetables. They also eat worms, grubs, dig holes, and	Avoid leaving pet and human food out, clean up wood and brush piles. Dogs can help deter raccoons

	they will eat your chickens if given a chance.	from coming into garden in general. Trap and relocate or kill.
Rodents	Eating nuts and seeds. They'll nibble on plants and roots that are sticking out of the ground.	Traps, clean up around garden, predator urines and cats are all helpful in getting rid of rodents. Invite owls by making nesting sites and snakes with rock piles.
Squirrels	They eat grains, seedlings, nuts, fruits, vines, tree bark, and dig around roots which can kill plants.	Dogs, traps, killing, and tree collars are all helpful tools in getting rid of squirrels.
Voles	They will eat greens, fruits, brassicas, roots, tomatoes, and damages trees.	Clean debris, fences a few feet high and a foot deep. Trapping and allowing, cats, inviting snakes with rock piles and owls with nest sites.

Unwanted Critters

Under the solutions column are some beneficial critters that help deal with the unwanted ones. Starting on page 37 are some suggestions on how to invite them.

Name	Damage	Solutions
Ants	Generally helpful to garden, but some ants can kill plants by tunneling around roots. Some ants also raise aphids and mealybugs.	Disrupting colony, pour boiling water on colony, plant mint and other aromatic herbs nearby.
Aphids	Transmitting diseases and fungi, sucking plant sap that causes misshaping, curling, stunted growth, and yellowing leaves.	Invite lady bugs, green lacewing, hoverflies, aphid midge, minute pirate bugs, big eyed bug, chalcid wasps, soldier beetles, damsel bugs, aphid wasps, assassin bugs. Plant alliums, mints, onions, garlic, and catnip. Use marigolds and nasturtiums as trap crops.

		Spray off aphids with jet of water.
Armyworms	Skeletonized leaves, brown spotting, holes.	Invite parasitic wasps, damsel bug, lacewings, minute pirate bugs, big-eyed bugs, assassin bugs. Invite birds with feeders and baths. Hand picking.
Asparagus beetles	Eating plant tips, devour fern like leaves.	Hand picking, removing plant residue before winter, and invite parasitic wasps.
Blister beetles	Skeletonized leaves	Hand picking with gloves (can cause blisters when handled).
Brown stink bug	Scaring, sunken areas, deformed, spongy areas, and tissue damage on leaves.	Invite Samurai wasp, assassin bug, earwigs, green lacewing, hand picking, and killing eggs under leaves.
Cabbage loopers	Holes in leaves, bore through vegetable plants	Invite parasitic wasps, tachinid parasitoids,

	with heads.	trichogramma, yellow jackets, Copidosoma truncatella, Hyposoter exiguae. Row covers. Black light and pheromone traps, whack.
Cabbage worms	Irregular holes in plant leaves. Might eventually eat whole plant.	Invite vespid wasp, birds, Apanteles glomeratus, Microplitis plutella, tachinid flies, Trichogramma. Handpick and kill eggs, whack.
Canker worm	Skeletonized leaves, biting into fruit.	Hot pepper and garlic oil spray, banding trees.
False chinch bugs	Wilting, curling, and possible plant decline under extreme cases.	Invite big-eyed bugs, ants, Geocoris uliginosus, striped earwig, Labidura riparia, ground beetles.
Colorado potato beetle	Eats all plant foliage.	Invite green lacewings, predatory stink

		bugs, ground beetles, spined soldier bug, and tachinid fly. Crop rotation. Heavy straw mulching. Hand picking and killing eggs.
Corn earworms	Consume corn tassels and bore into the tops of corn.	Invite tachinid flies, lady beetle, big-eyed bugs, Hippodamia convergens, green lacewing, Trichogramma wasps, and birds. Drop mineral oil on corn tops. Pull back wrapper leaves and hand pick.
Cutworms	Chewing on stems, sometimes completely severing plant. Holes in leaves.	Invite ground beetles, birds, nematodes, parasitic wasps, Ground cover, toilet roll paper collars, night handpick.
Diamond-back moths	Eats all but the foliage's veins. Can disrupt head	Inviting parasitic wasps, ground beetles,

	formation in cabbage family plants.	true bugs, syrphid fly, and spiders. Crop diversity. Irrigation lessens adult population. Using collards and mustards as trap crops.
Earwig (somewhat beneficial in that they eat mites and aphids)	Eat seedlings, annual flowers, corn silks, and some soft fruits.	Use traps with fish oil or vegetable oil and bacon grease, rolled up newspaper or corrugated cardboard: empty in the morning.
Flea beetle	Tiny pits and holes in leaves.	Invite ground beetles and parasitic wasps. Intercropping, regular soil cultivation, and cleaning up fall debris.
Fungus gnat	Damage roots, stunt plant.	Invite steinernema nematodes, predatory mites, hunter flies, and Bacillus

		thuringiensis. Yellow sticky traps, raw potato pieces in soil to trap and discard.
Gypsy moths	Feeds on tree leaves. Excessive consumption kills trees.	Invite tachinid flies, ground beetles, and Trichogramma wasps. Bands. Kill larva. Clean debris.
Japanese beetles	Skeletonized leaves, eats flowers, and larva will eat some roots.	Invite parasitic nematodes, parasitic wasps, and parasitic flies. Handpick or shake off beetles in morning and drown in soapy water. Row cover. Trap crop with geraniums.
Leaf hopper	Feeding on leaves causing pale or brown coloring, and causing shoots to curl and die. Black moldy spotting.	Invite mantids, dragonflies, green lacewings, minute pirate bugs, black hunter thrips, lady beetles, predaceous

		mites, some spiders, as well as parasitic wasps.
Leafminers	Stippled lines on foliage.	Inviting parasitic wasps. Row covers.
Mealybugs	Slow plant growth, leaf and fruit dropping off, twigs dying, affect fruit quality and taste.	Invite parasitic wasps, lady beetles, lacewings, mealybug destroyers. Knocking them off with a jet of water.
Mexican bean beetles	Skeletonized leaves, reducing yields. Will consume flowers and pods.	Invite spined soldier bugs, assassin bugs, tachinid fly, and parasitic wasps. Use soybeans as a trap crop.
Pickle worm	Eating blossoms and vines and digging into squash and melon fruits.	Invite soldier beetles, coleopteran, parasitoids, braconidae, trichogramma. Compost all plant materials, plant earlier varieties to avoid

		infestation, destroy leaves that are curled with pupate inside. Row covers.
Potato tuber worm	Feeding on stems and leaves; burrowing into tubers.	Invite parasitoids and braconidae. Plant early varieties, heavy mulch. Row covers. Compost all left over plant material. Compost volunteer plants.
Root knot Nematode	Injuring roots and causing galls which wilts and stunts plant growth.	Letting beds go fallow, crop rotation, preemptive soil treatment, soil solarization (wetting soil and covering with clear plastic to heat soil for a month or so), plant French marigolds, organic amendments such as compost

		and manure limit damage.
Root maggots	Holes and tunnels in roots, plants can wilt, turn yellow, and die under extreme infestation.	Invite predator nematodes, rove beetles. Spread diatomaceous earth around seedlings, use row covers, crop rotation, and destroy infested plants. Destroy eggs in soil around plants. Use collars around plants. Sticky traps.
Slug and snails	Destroyers of all that is good in the garden. Besides deer, slugs are my most troublesome guest. Eats most everything. Will destroy greens, especially seedlings. Irregular holes and slime on leaves.	I have found hand picking at night is the most effective control. Toss slugs in soapy water. Invite toads with toad homes and water ponds. Invite ground beetles, snakes, turtles, and birds. Lavender, rosemary, sage, ferns, California

		poppies, nasturtiums. Mulch with aromatic herbs. Liquid traps: cups with beer/yeast water buried to the top of container will attract and drown slugs. Barriers such as copper flashing.
Spider mites	Suck juices from underside of leaves, often killing leaves and stunting plants. Stunting fruit.	Invite predatory mites, lady beetles, minute pirate bugs, lacewings, spider mite destroyer, assassin bugs, ghost ants. Blast mites with jet of water.
Spittlebugs	Sucking plant sap, weakening plants. Getting their spittle everywhere.	Kill nymphs in spittle mass. Generally not too harmful to plants.
Squash borers	Tunnel into vines to eat. Any leaves that are part of vine wither and die.	Inviting parasitic wasps and parasitic nematodes. Compost plant

		materials at end of season to minimize later infestations. Fill yellow container with water to trap and drown borers. Row covers. Remove borers from vine early on by thinly slicing into small holes and killing borer. Spread black pepper, wood ash, or diatomaceous earth around early vines. Covering stems with something to prevent borers from getting in.
Squash bug	Sucks plant juices while excreting saliva toxins into plant. This causes the leaves and vines to blacken and die. Fruits do not produce.	Invite parasitic wasps, tachinid flies, and wasp egg parasitoids. Hand pick bugs and crush eggs. Row covers. Clean debris around garden.

Stink bug	Sucks juices from plant parts.	Invite birds, bats, some spiders, assassin bugs, predatory stink bugs, minute pirate bugs, lacewings, lady beetles, toads, praying mantis, and parasitic flies.
Tarnished plant bug	Sucks on plant juices and excretes toxic saliva into plant causing leaf distortion, falling buds, and tip death. Spreads plant diseases.	Invite minute pirate bugs, big-eyed bugs, damsel bugs, Row covers.
Tent caterpillars	Cover portions of tree in web like nests. Larva feed on leaves. Can totally defoliate trees.	Invite parasitic wasps, hymenoptera egg parasites, coleopteran, dermaptera, spined soldier bugs, frogs, and birds. Pull out nests with nails hammered through a stick by winding nest around it. Burn

		nests.
Thrips	Suck juices out of plant parts, leaving silvery speckled/streaks on leaves. Stunting plants and damaging fruits.	Invite predatory thrips, minute pirate bugs, lady beetles, predatory mites, and lacewings. Use yellow sticky traps to catch or reflective mulch to blind bugs from seeing plants.
Tomato hornworm	Eat leaves, stems, and fruits of nightshade family. Complete defoliation.	Invite trichogramma wasps, lady beetles, lacewings, braconoid, and hyposoter exiguae. Crop rotations. Spread diatomaceous earth around plants. Handpick and destroy bugs. Compost all plant material at end of season. Till in the spring to kill off most

		larva.
Weevils	Feed on foliage making leaves have ragged look and sometimes notched twigs. Larva feed on roots. Plants wilt and die.	Invite parasitic nematodes, parasitic wasps, some spiders, ground beetles, bluebirds, warblers, and wrens. Spread diatomaceous earth around plants.
Whiteflies	Suck plant juices causing them to weaken and sometimes die in extreme cases. Spreads viral diseases.	Invite parasitic wasps, lacewings, minute pirate bugs, big-eyed bugs, lady beetles, Harmonia axyridis, and predatory beetles. Yellow sticky plant traps. Reflective mulch.
Wireworm	Bore into roots, tubers, and bulbs, stunting and killing plants.	Invite parasitic nematodes, and birds. Till up 6-8 inches of soil to make it inhospitable. Crop rotations. Bury half of a

		potato 6 inches in soil to attract wireworms. Check after a few days and destroy infected tubers.

Corn, cucumber, & white clovers

VI
WANTED GUESTS

Name	Inviting	Benefits
Ambush bug	Wooded areas, asters, goldenrod, white and yellow flowers	Eats flies, butterflies & bees sadly, as well as many unwanted bugs
Aphid midge	Queen Anne's Lace, dill, thyme, wild mustard, groundcovers, wildflowers, shrubs, shelter from strong winds, water source	Eats aphids
Aphidius Wasp	Wherever aphids are	Eats aphids
Assassin bug	Trees and shrubs, goldenrod, ground covers	Eats aphids, asparagus beetle, bees sadly, and other flying insects
Bees	Flowers	Pollinators
Big-eyed bug	Ground cover, clovers, alfalfa, potatoes, pigweed, golden rod	Eats aphids, leafhoppers, caterpillars, chinch bugs, spider mites

Braconid wasps	Carrot family plants, cabbage family plants, corn, yarrow, small flowers with high nectar content	Eats aphids hornworms, webworms, European corn borers, cabbage maggots, diamondback moths, tomato hornworms, armyworms
Butterflies	Flowers in general, sunflowers, hollyhocks, lupine, milkweed, butterfly bush	Pollinators
Chalcid Wasps	Throughout garden flowers, leaf litter	Eats moths, flies, aphids, butterflies, beetles, scale, nematodes, whiteflies, leafhoppers, caterpillars
Damsel bug	Ground cover, fields, caraway, spearmint, fennel, clovers, alfalfa, goldenrod	Eats caterpillars, mites, aphids, cabbage worms, leafhoppers, plant bugs
Narrow Wing Damselfly	Water surfaces	Eats aphids, Mosquitos

Dragonflies	Ponds, tall grass, aquatic plants, buttonbush, perennials	Eats flies, mosquitoes, gnats, aphids
Fireflies	Decaying bark, garden debris	Eats many unwanted insects, slugs, snails
Ground beetles	Rocks, logs, compost piles, perennials, goldenrod, pigweed, groundcovers	Eats aphids, cabbage worms, Colorado potato beetles, cutworms, diamondback moths, gypsy moth, spider mites, asparagus beetle, tent caterpillar, flea beetles, root maggots, slugs, snails, cabbage maggots, caterpillars
Hoverflies	Yarrow, dill, caraway, coriander, Queen Anne's Lace, fennel, feverfew, English	Eats aphids, corn earworms, corn borers, thrips, leafhoppers, mealybugs, caterpillars. It's

	lavender, lemon balm, pennyroyal, spearmint, wild bergamot, parsley, zinnias	also a pollinator
Ichneumon wasp	Parsley, tansy, lovage, dill, sweet cicely, Queen Anne's Lace, carrots, flowering cover crops	Eats moths, Diamondback grubs, various caterpillars, European corn borers, cabbage moths
Brown lacewing	Woods and fields	Eats aphids, mealybugs, and other soft bodied insects
Green lacewing	Dill, corn, yarrow, caraway, cosmos, carrots, coriander, Queen Anne's Lace, fennel, tansy, sunflowers, dandelion	Eats aphids, whiteflies, leafhoppers, mealybugs, cabbage worms, cutworms, caterpillars, loopers, potato beetles, spider mites
Ladybugs	Alfalfa, dandelion, goldenrod, daisies, zinnias, dill, fennel, yarrow, lilacs,	Eats aphids, thrips, mites, mealybugs, scale, corn earworm larva

	coriander, marigold, tansy, hairy vetch	
Mealybug destroyer	Fennel, dill, sunflowers, goldenrod	Eats mealybugs
Minute pirate bug	Alfalfa, daisies, caraway, corn, clover, vetch, cosmos, fennel, spearmint, marigolds, goldenrod, cinquefoil, coneflowers	Eats aphids, thrips, spider mites, whiteflies, spider mites, leafhoppers, corn earworm eggs
Parasitic wasps	Yarrow, dill, caraway, Queen Anne's Lace, fennel, lemon balm, parsley, pennyroyal, marigold, tansy, zinnia, daisies, ground cover	Eats aphids, hornworms, corn borers, armyworms, whiteflies, leafhoppers, caterpillars, and many others
Praying mantis	Tall grass, shrubs, dill, marigolds	Eats, beetles, caterpillars, moths, crickets, grasshoppers, and many more
Predatory mites	Bell peppers, strawberries,	Eats thrips and spider mites.

	greenhouse plants, corn, cane fruits, mint	
Robber fly	Decaying wood, leaf mold	Eats maggots, grubs, butterflies, grasshoppers, flies, and some beneficial insects unfortunately
Rove beetles	Compost piles, mulches, rocks, ground cover, alfalfa, clovers	Eats aphids, mites, flies, nematodes, and cabbage maggots
Soldier beetles	Daisies, cosmos, sunflowers, goldenrod, zinnias, marigolds, milkweed, catnip, perennials	Eats aphids, grasshopper eggs, cucumber beetle
Spiders	Large plants, trees, shrubs, flower heads	Eats lots of things (good and bad)
Spined soldier bug	Perennials, tansy	Eats Colorado potato beetle, caterpillars, Mexican bean beetle,

		European corn borer, corn earworms, armyworms, imported cabbageworms, sawfly, and some beneficials
Tachinid fly	Dill, parsley, lemon balm, Queen Anne's Lace, carrots, tansy	Eats gypsy moth, cabbage loopers, armyworms, cucumber beetles, Japanese beetles, armyworms, cutworms, sawflies, tent caterpillars, squash bugs, corn borers, potato beetles, and much more
Tiger beetle	Sand, groundcover, dry garden areas	Eats ants, flies, caterpillars, aphids, and grasshoppers
Trichogramma Wasps	Tansy, Queen Anne's Lace, coriander, parsley, carrots	Eats European corn borer, light brown apple moth, cabbageworms,

		corn earworms, cabbage loopers

In addition to growing specific plants some other things you can do to invite welcomed guests are to have a pile of rocks for snakes, lizards, and other beneficial creatures, make toad and frog homes, have ponds and other water sources, insect and bird baths and houses, bird feeders, bat houses, carpenter bee homes, bee logs, and owl nesting sites are a few things that can be done.

VII
PLANTS

Plant Name

Name: *Scientific name*
Family: plant family
Germination: time it takes to germinate
Height: how tall plant gets
Root Depth: how deep roots grow in optimal conditions
pH: optimal levels
Spacing: first numbers are between plants, second numbers are between rows
Needs: whatever special needs a plant may have
Companions: plants that are beneficial in some way or another. There are many benefits that come with companion planting. The five I focus on are:

- Pest deterrent (P)
- Disease deterrent (D)
- Trap crops (T) are plants that attracts unwanted insects instead of one's chosen crop.
- Enhancing flavor, growth, and/or yield (E)
- Inviting beneficials (I) to pollinate and eat unwanted guests

Detrimental: plants that are not so good to be around
Problems: diseases, pests, and other issues that might arise.

Asparagus

Name: *Asparagus officinalis*
Family: Asparagus

Germination: 14-20 days
Height: 3-8'
Root Depth: 3-4'
pH: 6.5-7.5
Spacing: 18-20" x 3-4'
Needs: Mulch, side dress with compost or manure, water regularly, full sun, deep soil.
Companions: Asters (I), basil (P), coriander (I, P), cosmos (I), dill (I, P), horseradish (D, P), marigolds (I, P), parsley (I, P), strawberries, tomatoes.
Detrimental: Alliums
Problems: Aphids, asparagus beetle, asparagus miners, asparagus rust, fusarium wilt, crown rot, cucumber beetle, cutworms, rust, thrips.

Beans

Name: *Phaseolus vulgaris*
Family: Pea
Germination: 1-4 days
Height: 2-6' depending on beans
Root Depth: 16-24" and 24-36" spreading.
pH: 6.0-6.8
Spacing: Different for each variety
Needs: Full sun, side dress with compost later in the season.
Companions: Anise (P, I, E), basil (P), beets, borage (P, I, E), cabbage, carrots (I), catnip (I, P), cauliflower, celery, chamomile (I, E), chard, collards, corn (support), dill (I, P), kale, marigold (I, P), nasturtium (P, T), peas (E), potatoes, radish (I, T), rosemary (I, P), sage (P), savory (E), squash, strawberries, French tarragon (I, E).
Detrimental: Alliums, beets (pole beans), gladiolus, and sunflowers depending on bean

variety.

Problems: Bean rust, skeletonized leaves from Mexican bean beetles, seedcorn maggots, root rot nematodes, wireworms, potato leafhoppers, tarnished plant bugs, bean aphids, bean mosaic, curly top virus, downy mildew, mites, bean leaf beetles, flea beetles, green stink bugs, bean weevils, seedcorn maggots, wireworms, leafminers, mites, bean leaf beetle.

Beets

Name: *Beta vulgaris*
Family: Amaranth
Germination: 5-8 days
Height: 4-12"
Root Depth: 16-24"
pH: 6.0-7.5
Spacing: 1" deep, 4" all around
Needs: Full sun to partial shade, cooler weather, loose, well drained, and fertile soil.
Companions: Arugula (T), bush beans, cabbage family members, calendula (I), potted catnip (P, I, E) garlic (E, P), kohlrabi, lettuce, potted mint (P), onions (P).
Detrimental: Pole beans
Problems: Tough and flavorless due to heat or lack of watering, flea beetles, aphids, leaf-spot disease can be avoided by rotation and avoiding places where beets, spinach, and Swiss chard were grown the year before, leafminers, aphids, downy mildew, beet armyworms, curly top virus, scab.

Broccoli

Name: Brassica oleracea
Family: Cabbage
Germination: 4-6 days
Height: 18-36"
Root Depth: 18-36"
pH: 6.0-7.0
Spacing: 1.5'
Needs: Full sun, cool season, very fertile soil, mulching, calcium.
Companions: Anise (P, I), asters (I), beets, bush beans, cabbage family, calendula (I), carrots, celery, chamomile (I, E), chervil (I, P), cucumbers, dill (I, P), hyssop (I, T), lettuce, marigolds (I, P), mint (I, P), nasturtium (P, T), onions (P), parsley (I, P), potatoes, rosemary (I, P), sage (P), thyme (I), zinnia (I).
Detrimental: Pole beans, mustards, peppers, strawberries, tomatoes.
Problems: Cabbageworms, cabbage loopers, diamondback moths, aphids, rabbits, deer, fungal rot.

Brussels Sprouts

Name: *Brassica oleracea*
Family: Cabbage or Mustard
Germination: 7-12 days
Height: 2-3'
Root Depth: 18-36"
pH: 5.5-6.8
Spacing: 15-18" x 24-24"
Needs: Full to partial sun, heavy feeders needing lots of compost or well-rotted manure, mulching.
Companions: Artichoke, beets, cabbage, calendula

(I), carrots (I), cauliflower, celery (E), chamomile (I, E), chervil (I, P), collards, cucumbers, dill (I, P), fennel (I), geraniums (I, P), hyssop (I, T), kale, marigolds (I, P), potted mint (P), nasturtium (P, T), onions (E, P), parsley (I, P), peas (E), rosemary (I, P), sage (P), thyme (I), potted wormwood (P), zinnia (I).

Detrimental: Strawberries, tomatoes.

Problems: Cabbage worms and loopers, diamondback moths, cutworms, maggots, root maggot, flea beetles, club root, black rot, blackleg, yellows.

Cabbage

Name: *Brassica oleracea*
Family: Cabbage or Mustard
Germination: 4-14 days
Height: 12-24"
Root Depth: 1-5'
pH: 6.0-6.8
Spacing: 15" x 24-30"
Needs: Heavy feeders needing rotted manure and compost, mulch, good drainage.
Companions: Asters (I), borage (P, I, E), carrot families (I), chervil (I, P), clover (E, I), dill (P, I), kale, marigolds (P), mint (P), pennyroyal (P), sage (P), thyme (I), wormwood (P).
Detrimental: Grapes, marigolds (help with pest problems but reduce growth due to allelopathic properties), nasturtiums (attract cabbage flea beetle), peppers, rue, strawberries, tomatoes.
Problems: Cutworms, aphids, cabbage loopers, root maggots, clubroot, mildew, diamondback moths, aphids, fungal diseases, blight, black rot,

49

harlequin bugs, striped flea beetle, wire stem, fusarium yellows, blight, downy mildew, thrips

Carrots

Name: *Daucus carota*
Family: Parsley or Carrot
Germination: 7-21 days
Height: 12-18"
Root Depth: 2-4'
pH: 5.5-7.0
Spacing: 2-3" x 16-30"
Needs: Loose, rock free soil, compost, full sun.
Companions: Beets, broccoli, calendula (P, I), caraway (P, I, E), chamomile (P, I), chives (D, I, P), leeks (P), lettuce, onions (P), peas (E), peppers, radishes, rosemary (P), sage (P), tomatoes (P).
Detrimental: Anise (poor growth), dill (poor growth).
Problems: Aster yellows, aphids, tarnished plant bugs, carrot rust fly, carrot beetle, carrot weevils, leafhoppers, cutworms, aphids, root knot nematodes, wireworms, fungal and bacterial diseases.

Cauliflower

Name: *Brassica oleracea*
Family: Cabbage
Germination: 8-10 days
Height: 18-24"
Root Depth: 12-18"
pH: 5.5-7.5
Spacing: 12-15" x 24-46"
Needs: Heavy feeder needing compost and or well-rotted manure, full sun, well-drained soil,

mulch.

Companions: Celery (E), chervil (I, P), dill (I, P), potted mint (P), nasturtium (P, T), onions (P, E), pennyroyal (P), potatoes (E), sage (P), thyme (I), zinnias (I).

Detrimental: Grapes.

Problems: Aphids, cabbage root maggots, cabbage loopers, clubroot, downy mildew.

Celery

Name: *Apium graveolens*
Family: Carrot
Germination: 7-10 days
Height: 15-18"
Root Depth: 6-12"
pH: 6.0-7.0
Spacing: 6-8"-18-36"
Needs: Lots of water, full sun to partial shade, potassium, fish emulsion.
Companions: Beans, cabbage, calendula (I), cauliflower, chives (D, I, P), collards, cosmos (I), daisy (I), garlic (P), kale, leeks (P), potatoes (E), zinnias (I).
Detrimental: Asters (invites insects that can cause celery leaf damage) corn, lettuce.
Problems: Slugs, parsley/celery worms, aphids, carrot rust fly, celery mosaic, fungal diseases, fasarium yellows, blight.

Collards

Name: *Brassica oleracea*
Family: Cabbage or Mustard
Germination: 4-10 days
Height: 24-34"

Root Depth: 2-3'
pH: 6.0-6.5
Spacing: 18"
Needs: Full sun, well-drained soil, mulching.
Companions: Beans (E), brassica family members, chervil (I, P), onions (P), tomatoes (P).
Detrimental: Grapes, marigold (reduce growth due to allelopathic properties).
Problems: Flea beetle, cabbage worms, black leg, leaf spot, black rot, rhizoctonia.

Corn

Name: *Zea mays*
Family: Corn
Germination: 10-14 days
Height: 5-16"
Root Depth: 4-7'
pH: 5.5-7.0
Spacing: 10-15" x 36-42"
Needs: Heavy feeder, needs lots of compost and well-aged manure, full sun, mulch (squash does this nicely), steady water supply.
Companions: Beans and peas (E, I, P), white clovers (locking in nitrogen and acts as a living mulch), cucumbers, nasturtium (P, T), potatoes, radishes, soybeans (E), squash, sunflower (D, I), tansy (I, P).
Detrimental: Quack grass, tomatoes (encourage earworms).
Problems: Borer, birds, earworms, army worms, cutworms, rootworms, dwarf mosaic, seedcorn beetle and maggots, wireworms, aphids, flea beetle, rust, blight, pill bugs, raccoons, deer when plant is young, bacterial wilt, corn blight, sap beetle.

Cucumber

Name: *Cucumis sativus*
Family: Gourd
Germination: 7-10 days
Height: 1' +
Root Depth: 2-3'
pH: 5.5-7.5
Spacing: 12" x 2'
Needs: Generous watering (avoid wetting lower stem), likes the sun but will tolerate some shade.
Companions: Spiny amaranth (T, I, E), beans and peas (E), cabbage (E), carrots (I), celery, red clovers (I, E), corn (E), dill (I, P), lettuce, marigold (I, P), radish (E, P), sunflower (I), tomatoes.
Detrimental: Potatoes, sage and other strong aromatic herbs.
Problems: Cucumber beetle, gray squash bugs, bacterial wilt, powdery mildew, squash vine borers, nematodes, mosaic, aphids, downy and powdery mildews, squash borers, angular leaf spot, alernaria blight, black rot, scab.

Eggplant

Name: *Solanum melongena*
Family: Nightshade
Germination: 7-14 days
Height: 24-30"
Root Depth: 4-7'
pH: 6.0-7.0
Spacing: 18-30" x 24-38"
Needs: Heavy feeder, full sun, heat.
Companions: Amaranth (T, I, E), basil (P), bush beans, green beans (E), dill (I, P), lettuce, marigolds (P), peppers, redroot pigweed (E, P), tarragon (P, I,

E), thyme (I), tomatoes, peas (E).
Detrimental: Pole beans, fennel, potatoes.
Problems: Flea beetle, cutworm, spider mites, fusarium wilt, lace bugs, blister beetle, Colorado potato beetle, blight.

Garlic

Name: *Allium sativum*
Family: Amaryllis
Germination: cloves sprout in 2-8 weeks
Height: 1-3'
Root Depth: 2-24"
pH: 5.5-7.5
Spacing: 4-6" x 1.5-2'
Needs: Planted in fall, loose well-drained soil, full sun.
Companions: Cabbage family members, eggplant, lettuce and other salad greens, tomatoes.
Detrimental: Hurtful to legumes.
Problems: Onion thrips, white rot, onion maggots, cutworms, aphids, pink root, fusarium bulb rot, lesser bulb flies, wireworms, leaf blight, rust, onion smudge, neck rot.

Kale

Name: *Brassica oleracea*
Family: Cabbage or Mustard
Germination: 7-10 days
Height: 12-24"
Root Depth: 6-12"
pH: 6.0-7.5
Spacing: 15-18" x 24-46"
Needs: Rich, well-draining soil, full sun.
Companions: Beans (E), beets, Brussel sprouts,

cabbage family members, calendula (I), celery, chamomile (I, E), chervil (I, P), cucumbers, dandelion (I), dill (I, P), leeks (P), lettuce, marigolds (I, P), mint (P), nasturtium (P, T), onions (P), peas (E), potatoes, rosemary (I, P), sage (P).
Detrimental: Grapes, tomatoes.
Problems: Slugs, aphids, cabbage loopers, cabbage worms, harlequin bug, flea beetle, clubroot.

Leeks

Name: *Allium porrum*
Family: Amaryllis
Germination: 5-7 days
Height: 15-36"
Root Depth: 8-18"
pH: 6.0-7.5
Spacing: 5-7" x 11"
Needs: Sun to partial shade, hill up to blanch stems.
Companions: Cabbage family members, carrots (I), celery, lettuce, onions (P), tomatoes.
Detrimental: Legumes
Problems: Onion fly, smut, pink root.

Lettuce and other Greens

Name: *Lactuca sativa*
Family: Sunflower or Aster
Germination: 3-7 days
Height: 6-12"
Root Depth: 18-36"
pH:6.0-7.5
Spacing: 6-12" x 12-14"
Needs: Sun when it is cold and shade when it's hot, loose well-draining soil.

Companions: Beets, carrots (I), chervil (I, P), chives (D, I, P), cucumbers, garlic (P), hyssop (I, T), leeks (P), onions (P), radishes (P), sage (P), strawberries, sunflower (I).

Detrimental: Celery, parsley.

Problems: Slugs, slugs, slugs: urrrrrr. I've found radishes help because the slugs seem to be attracted to them more than the lettuce at first. Hand collecting at night and in the morning seems to be the best option in addition to spreading used coffee grounds around plants. Rabbits, aphids, snails, cutworms, mildew, viral disease, wireworms, tarnished plant bugs, leafhoppers, thrips, aster yellows, mosaic virus, bottom rot, flea beetle, powdery and downy mildews, leafminers.

Melons

Name: *Cucumis melo (muskmelons) Citrullus lanatus (watermelon)*

Family: Gourd

Germination: 4-10 days

Height: 24"

Root Depth: 2-4'

pH: 6.0-7.0

Spacing: 2-4' x 5-7'

Needs: Lots of compost or aged manure.

Companions: Beets, corn (E), peas (E), marigolds (I, P), nasturtium (P, T), radishes (P), sunflower (I).

Detrimental: Potatoes.

Problems: Squash borers, squash bugs, powdery mildew, bacteria wilt, cucumber beetle, mites, mildews and fungal diseases, mosaic, aphids, leaf blight, fusarium and bacterial wilts, scab.

Mushrooms

Adding manure, mulch, and compost to the garden will naturally bring in mushrooms of all different sorts. Most mushrooms are beneficial for the garden. They help break down matter into delicious loam that plants relish. They increase water and nutrient uptake, improve disease resistance, reduce weather stress, improve soil structure, help retain moisture, and accelerate plant growth rates. There are groups of mushrooms called entomopathogenic fungi that act as a pesticide while still others help fight off some common plant pathogens like the Trichogerma species. There are a few mushrooms that are not good for the garden in that they consume more than they give. One group comes from the Armillaria family. Three edible mushrooms that will grow right in the vegetable patch are Shaggy Mane (Coprinus comatus), the Elm Oyster (Hypsizgus ulmanarius), and the delicious Wine Caps (Stropharia rugosoannulata).

Onions

Name: *Allium cepa*
Family: Amaryllis
Germination: 6-12 days
Height: 15-36"
Root Depth: 18-36"
pH: 6.0-7.5
Spacing: 3-5" x 12-18"
Needs: Weeded, full sun.
Companions: Beets, cabbage family members, carrots (I), celery, chamomile (I, E), lettuce, potatoes, pumpkins, radish (I, T), savory (E), squash, strawberries, tomatoes.

Detrimental: Legumes, parsley.
Problems: Thrips, onion maggots, basal rot, pink root, cutworms, aphids, fusarium bulb rot, rust, smut, mildew, white rot, lesser bulb flies, wireworms, leaf blight, onion smudge, neck rot.

Parsnip

Name: *Pastinaca sativa*
Family: Carrot
Germination: 14-20 days
Height: 30-70"
Root Depth: 10-20"
pH: 6.0-7.5
Spacing: 3-5" x 18-24"
Needs: Full sun, well-draining soil.
Companions: Corn, garlic (P), legumes (E), marigolds (I, P), melons, onions, peas (E), peppers, potatoes, radish (I, T), squashes.
Detrimental: Carrot family members because they invite carrot rust fly, beetles, and weevils.
Problems: Aster yellows, aphids, tarnished plant bugs, carrot rust fly, carrot beetle, carrot weevils, leafhoppers, cutworms, root knot nematodes, wireworms, fungal and bacterial diseases, parsnip canker.

Peas

Name: Pisum sativum
Family: Pea
Germination: 8-10 days
Height: 2-6'
Root Depth: 1-3'
pH: 6.0-7.0
Spacing: 2-4" x 18-48"

Needs: Full sun.
Companions: Anise (P, I), beans (E), carrots (I), corn, cucumbers, potatoes, radishes, turnips.
Detrimental: Alliums.
Problems: Deer, powdery mildew, aphids, pea weevils, root rot, seedcorn maggots, cutworms, potato leafhoppers, tarnish plant bugs, pea aphids, wilts, mosaic, mites, downy and powdery mildews, blight, leadfminers, cucumber bee.

Peppers

Name: *Capsicum frutescens*
Family: Nightshade
Germination: 14-21 days
Height: 2-3'
Root Depth: 8-48"
pH: 6.0-7.0
Spacing: 12-24" x 18-36"
Needs: Heavy feeders, full sun.
Companions: Alliums (P), amaranth (T, I, E), asparagus, basil (P), beans (E), borage (P, I, E), carrots (I), celery, dill (I, P), garlic (P), lettuce, marigolds (I, P), nasturtium (P, T), parsley (I, P), redroot pigweed (E, P), roses, sage (P), Sweet Annie (I).
Detrimental: Kohlrabi, fennel, potatoes.
Problems: Aphids, cutworms, nematodes, fusarium and verticillium wilts, bacterial wilt, leafminers, flea beetles, hornworms, pepper maggots, European corn borers, earworms, pepper weevils, tobacco mosaic virus, mites.

Potatoes

Name: *Solanum tuberosum*
Family: Nightshade
Germination: 14-28 days
Height: 23-36"
Root Depth: 18-24"
pH: 4.8-6.0
Spacing: 10-12" x 20-26"
Needs: Full sun, mulch (I like spoiled straw)
Companions: Amaranth (T, I, E), basil (P), beans (E), cabbage, catnip (I, E), coriander (I, P), corn, eggplant, horseradish (D, P), marigold (I, P), nasturtium (P, T), parsley (I, P), peas (E), savory (E).
Detrimental: Cucumbers, pumpkins, raspberries, rosemary, squash, sunflower, tomatoes.
Problems: Colorado potato beetle, potato blight, potato scab, viral disease, flea beetle, aphids, early and late blight, fungal and bacterial infections, leafhoppers, aphids, white grubs, blister beetles, scab, root knot nematodes, wireworms, tuberworms.

Radish

Name: *Raphnus sativus*
Family: Cabbage
Germination: 4-7 days
Height: 2-12"
Root Depth: 3-6"
pH: 5.8-7.0
Spacing: 1"-2" x 8-12"
Needs: Full sun to partial shade.
Companions: Cabbage family members, lettuce, carrots (I), chervil (I, P), cucumbers, garlic (P),

legumes (E), marigolds (I, P), nasturtium (P, T), onions (P), peas (E).
Detrimental: Hyssop, grapes.
Problems: Cabbage maggots, flea beetles, slugs on leaves, rodents, clubroot, scab, downy mildew.

Spinach

Name: *Spinacia olercea*
Family: Spinach
Germination: 7-10 days
Height: 4-12"
Root Depth: 1-5'
pH: 6.5-7.5
Spacing: 6-12" x 12-14"
Needs: Fertile, well-draining soil.
Companions: Cabbage family members, celery, eggplant, onion (P), peas (E), peppers, strawberries, borage (P, I, E), cosmos (I), dill (I, P), yarrow (I, P).
Detrimental: Potatoes.
Problems: Spinach leafminers, aphids, slugs, leafhoppers, fusarium wilt, aphids, white rust, flea beetle, downy mildew, mosaic virus, various caterpillars.

Squash

Name: *Cucurbita pepo*
Family: Gourd
Germination: 6-12 days
Height: 12-40"
Root Depth: 1-6'
pH: 5.5-7.5
Spacing: 24-28" x 36-60"
Needs: Full sun, heavy feeder.
Companions: Basil (P), beans (E), buckwheat (I,

E), catnip (I, P), celery, clovers (E), corn, fennel (I), marigold (I, P), mint (P), nasturtium (P, T), onions (P), oregano (I, P), radish (I, T), spinach, sunflower (I), thyme (I), tansy (I, P), yarrow (I, P), zucchini.
Detrimental: Potatoes.
Problems: Squash bugs and borers, downy and powdery mildew, cucumber beetle, mosaic virus, bacterial wilt, spider mites, pickleworms, aphids.

Sweet Potatoes

Name: *Ipomoea batatas*
Family: Morning glory
Germination: 2-5 days for slip root growth
Height: 12-15"
Root Depth: 1-6'
pH: 5.5-6.5
Spacing: 12-16" x 36-40"
Needs: Full sun.
Companions: Beets, dill (I), white hellebore (I), nasturtium (P, T), parsnips, thyme (I).
Detrimental: Squashes because of similar growing habits.
Problems: Sweet potato weevil, stem rot, scurf, black rot, nematodes, squash stinkbugs, rabbits, fusarium wilt, flea beetle, tortoise beetle, bacterial and fungal diseases, white grubs, cutworms.

Swiss Chard

Name: *Beta vulgaris*
Family: Amaranth
Germination: 4-7 days
Height: 12-24"
Root Depth: 8-12" can go up to 5' if not getting watered: turns leaves bitter.

pH: 6.0-7.0

Spacing: 12-18"

Needs: Moderate feeding, full sun to partial shade.

Companions: Alliums (P), beans (E), black eyed Susan's (I), cabbage family members, calendula (I), daisies (I), fennel (I), lettuce, spinach, Sweet Annie (I).

Detrimental: Corn, cucumber, melons.

Problems: Flea beetles, leaf miners, aphids, leaf-spot disease can be avoided by rotation and avoiding places where beets, spinach, and Swiss chard were grown the year before, downy mildew, beet armyworms, curly top virus, scab.

Tree Guilds

Permaculture Tree Guilds focus on companion planting with trees. There are at least six types of companion plants in Tree Guilds: attractors, repellers, mulchers, accumulators, fixers, and suppressors. *Attractors* invite pollinators and other beneficial critters like parasitic and predatory insects, frogs and toads, snakes and birds. Some good examples are bee balm, bird's foot trefoil, borage, buckwheat, chamomile, clover, cosmos, mustards, rue, umbelliferaes, and yarrow. *Repellers* are plants that repel or trap unwanted guests. A few good examples are mints, alliums, coriander, lemongrass, marigolds, foxglove to deter deer, and nasturtiums to trap aphids. *Mulchers* are plants that have a lot of bulk material that can be trimmed and used as a mulch around trees. A few good examples are comfrey, burdock, docks, weeds or grass clippings, artichokes, and rhubarb. *Accumulators* have deep roots that pull up nutrients for the tree to use by placing plant materials to break down around the tree's drip line. Some examples are dandelion, chicory, comfrey, borage, burdock, turnip, horseradish, and thistles. *Fixers* help fix nitrogen into the soil. Legumes like clover, beans, peas, alfalfa, vetch, and lupine are a few good examples. *Suppressors* suppress unwanted plants by outcompeting with them. A few examples are strawberries, creeping thyme, bulbs, mint family members, chickweed, purslane, buckwheat, and squashes.

Tomato

Name: *Lycopersicon esculentum*
Family: Nightshade
Germination: 5-10 days
Height: 3-15'
Root Depth: 8-60"
pH: 6.0-7.0
Spacing: 2'-3'
Needs: Fertile, well-drained soil in full sun.
Companions: Amaranth (T, I, E), asparagus, alliums (P), basil (P), beans (E), borage (P, I, E), carrots (I), celery, dill (I, P), lettuce, marigolds (I, P), parsley (I, P), nasturtium (P, T), redroot pigweed (E, P), roses, garlic (P), pot marigolds (I, P), sage (P), Sweet Annie (I).
Detrimental: Apricots, cabbage family members, eggplant, fennel, kohlrabi, peppers, potatoes (kind of).
Problems: Red spider mites, blossom end rot, tomato hornworms, Colorado potato beetles, flea beetles, fungal diseases, nematodes, cutworms, root knot nematodes, bacteria wilt and spot, stink bug,

tomato pinworms, tomato fruit worms, mites, blights, slugs and snails, various animals, aphids, tobacco mosaic virus, fusarium and verticillium wilts.

Tomatillos

Name: *Physalis philadelphica*
Family: Nightshade
Germination: 7-14 days
Height: 3-4'
Root Depth: 18-48"
pH: 6.0-7.0
Spacing: 18-24" x 3-4'
Needs: Full sun, fertile well-drained soil.
Companions: Alliums (P), basil (I, P), bush beans (E), calendula (I), carrots (I), celery, cucumbers, marigolds (I, P), mints (I, P), nasturtium (P, T), parsley (I, P), peppers.
Detrimental: Corn, dill, eggplant, fennel, kohlrabi, potatoes.
Problems: Anthracnose, bacterial leaf spot, root knot nematodes, mosaic, wilt, aphids, cutworms, slugs, spider mites, whitefly.

Turnips

Name: *Brassica rapa*
Family: Cabbage family
Germination: 3-5 days
Height: 6-18"
Root Depth: 16-24"
pH: 5.5-7.5
Spacing: 2-4" x 1-1.5'
Needs: Full sun, loose rich soil.
Companions: Beans (E), carrots (I), chard,

chamomile (I, E), dill (I, P), lettuce, fennel (I), onions (P), peas (E), radishes, vetch (E).
Detrimental: Potatoes
Problems: Cabbage maggots, slugs, flea beetle, clubroot, black rot, anthracnose, downy mildew.

Sunflower, kale, catnip, & nasturtiums

VIII
REFERENCE TABLES

The following statistics are averages based on optimal growing conditions. Refer to individual seed packets for growing information.

Plant Height

Feet	Plants
½-1.5	Arugula, kohlrabi, lettuce, beets, carrots, radish, spinach, endives, turnips
1-2.5	Leeks, onions, garlic, cabbage, cauliflower, chard, pumpkin, rutabaga, squash, kale, watermelon
2-3	Bush beans, beans, broccoli, Brussel sprouts, bell peppers, sweet potatoes
3-4	Hot peppers, bell peppers, tomatoes
4-6	Artichoke, asparagus, peas, some corns varieties, quinoa, tomatoes
6-12	Okra, other corn varieties

Root Depth

Feet	Plants
1	Radish and spinach
1-2	Garlic, onions, lettuce, peas, summer squash, strawberries
1.5-2.5	Turnips, carrots
2	Cabbage, cauliflower, celery, cucumber, green beans eggplant
2-3	Artichokes, peppers,

	potatoes, sweet potatoes, watermelons
3-4	Cantaloupe, tomatoes
3-5	Beets
4-5	Lima beans
6	Asparagus, sweet corn, and Swiss chard

Approximate Watering Needs

Gallons per week	Plants
½-1	Carrots, turnips
1-2	Beans, beets, broccoli, Brussels sprouts, cabbage, collards, cucumbers, kale, kohlrabi, melons, onions, parsnips, peas, radish, squash
2-3	Cabbage, celery, cauliflower, lettuce, peppers. spinach, chard, tomatoes

pH Levels

Levels	Plants
4.8-6.0	Potato
5.5-6.5	Sweet potato
5.5-7.0	Brussels sprouts, corn, carrots, radish
5.5-7.5	Cauliflower, cucumbers, garlic, squash, turnips

6.0-6.5	Collards
6.0-7.0	Beans, broccoli, cabbage, chard, celery, eggplant, muskmelons, peas, peppers, tomato, tomatillos
6.0-7.5	Beets, kale, leeks, lettuce, onions, parsnips
6.5-7.5	Asparagus, spinach

Feeding Needs

Level	Plants
Heavy	Artichokes, broccoli, celery, corn, cucumbers, eggplant, garlic, melons, parsnips, peppers, pumpkins, squash, strawberries, tomatoes
Moderate	Brussel sprouts, kale, broccoli, chard, collards, cauliflower, kohlrabi, lettuce, parsley, spinach
Light	Beets, carrots, garlic, horseradish, Jerusalem artichokes, potatoes, onions, leeks, radishes, sweet potatoes, turnips, tomatillos

Light Requirements

Hours	Plants
Shade (0-3)	Alpine strawberries, red and black huckleberries, rhubarb, gooseberries, currants, blackberries, hazelnuts, black raspberries, sour cherry, pawpaws
Dapple shade (3-4)	Arugula, cabbage, kale, endive, lettuce, spinach, parsley, red raspberry, scallions
Partial shade (4-6)	Beets, broccoli, carrots, cauliflower, coriander, leeks, onion, radishes, turnips, peas, potatoes
Full sun (6-8)	Artichokes, asparagus, beans, Brussels sprouts, cucumbers, eggplants, melons, peppers, squash, tomatoes, tomatillos

Temperature Preferences

Temperatures	Plants
Warm	Bush beans, chili peppers, cucumbers, corn, eggplant, melons, okra, potatoes, squashes, sweet peppers, tomatoes tomatillos

Cool	Beets, broccoli, cabbage carrots, cauliflower, chard, chives, kale, kohlrabi, leeks, lettuce, onions, parsley, peas, radish, spinach, turnips

Plant Spacing in Inches

Plant Name	Between Plants	Between Rows
Asparagus	24	36-48
Beets	2	12
Broccoli	12-24	24-36
Bush beans	3-6	24-30
Cabbage	15	12-24
Carrots	3-4	6
Chives	18	18
Corn	15	18-24
Cucumbers	12	48-60
Eggplants	24	24
Endives	12	12
Garlic	4	12
Lettuce	12-16	6-12
Onions	6	18
Peas	3	8-24
Peppers	24	18
Potatoes	6-12	10
Radishes	2-4	6-10
Squash	24	48
Tomatoes	12-24	36-48

Seasonal Garden Chores

Season	Chores
Spring	Repairs, prepare garden beds when warm, planting seeds, mulching, cold frames, weeding, check hoses, clean up greenhouse, dividing plants, hunting slugs, weeding, bare root planting (early), test and amend soil, adding compost and aged manure, cut out unwanted shoots, clean bird houses, support plants
Summer	Watering, succession planting, weeding, composting, mulching, cover crops, remove diseased foliage, side dressing with compost and/or aged manure, deadheading, harvesting, critter hunting, save seeds
Fall	Mulching, cover crops, pruning, planting, propagating cuttings, storing root crops, save seeds, creating leaf mold, composting, creating new garden beds, clean up fallen fruits and dead plant materials, amend soil (late), garden cleaning, plant garlic
Winter	Garden planning, order seeds, clean and sharpen tools, protect plants from harsh weather, tune motorized tools, mulching, make sure plants are protected, early indoor planting, repairs, pruning apples, pears, figs, grapes, and soft fruit bushes (early), check fencing, insulated water spigots, chit early potatoes, indoor sowing

Harvest Times

Days	Plants
25-30	Radish
45-60	Broccoli, beets, lettuce and other greens, spinach, turnips, cucumbers
55-75	Beans, cabbage, carrots, cauliflower, collard, peas
68-85	Muskmelons, eggplant, peppers, sweet corn, tomatoes, watermelons
80-90	Brussel sprouts
100-110	Fennel, pumpkins, sweet potatoes, onions
120-130	Parsnips

Plant Families

Family	Plants
Amaranthaceae Amaranth Family	Amaranth, Swiss chard, lamb's quarters, quinoa
Apiaceae/Unbelliferae Parsley or Carrot Family	Caraway. carrots, celery, chervil, cilantro, dill, fennel, lovage, parsley, parsnips, Queen Anne's Lace
Asparagacea Asparagus Family	Asparagus, agave
Asteracea Sunflower or Aster Family	Artichoke, chicory, endives, lettuce, sunflowers, Jerusalem artichokes

Brassicaceae/Cruciferae Cabbage or Mustard Family	Arugula, broccoli, Brussel sprouts, cabbage, cauliflower, Chinese cabbage, collards, garden cress, kale, kohlrabi, horseradish, mustard, radishes, rutabaga, turnips
Chenopodiaceae	Beets, Swiss chard, spinach
Cucurbitaceae Squash Family	Cantaloupes, cucumbers, summer squash, winter squash, pumpkins, watermelons, zucchini
Fabaceae Pea Family	Beans, peas, peanuts, alfalfa
Lamiaceae Mint Family	Anise hyssop, bee balm, mountain mint, spearmint, peppermint, basil, sage, rosemary, savory, marjoram, oregano, hyssop, thyme, lavender, etc...
Liliaceae Lily Family	Chives, garlic, garlic chives, leeks, onions, scallions, shallots
Poaceae Grasses	Corn, wheat, rice, barley, millet, bamboo, straw, sugarcane
Solanaceae Nightshade Family	Eggplants, tomatoes, peppers, potatoes, tomatillos

Cross-pollination

If you are saving seeds you need to know what will cross-pollinate. With all but corn, cross-pollination will not affect the taste or look of the current plant. The seeds produced on the other hand will reflect the genetics of the two parent plants. Generally a plant will only cross if they are of the same species, but squashes and a few other plants like to break the rules. Below is a basic list of what will cross.

Plants	Cross With
Asparagus	Wild Asparagus
Beans	Self-pollinating, small chance of crossing with other beans
Beets	Sugar beet, spinach beet, Swiss chard
Broccoli	Brussel sprouts, cabbage, cauliflower, collard greens, kale, kohlrabi
Brussel sprouts	Broccoli, cabbage, cauliflower, collard greens, kale, kohlrabi
Carrots	Queen Anne's Lace and other subspecies
Cabbage	Broccoli, Brussel sprouts, cauliflower, collard greens, kale, kohlrabi
Cauliflower	Broccoli, Brussel sprouts, cabbage, collard

	greens, kale, , kohlrabi
Corn	Sweet corn, popcorn, ornamental corns
Cucumbers	Pickling cucumbers, slicers, and burpless. Will not cross with melons or gourds.
Eggplant	Self-fertile
Garlic	Self-fertile
Melons	Honeydew, cantaloupe, canary melon, muskmelon, casabas
Onions	Rare cases of crossing between other Allium members.
Parsnip	Wild parsnip
Pea	Self-pollinating
Peppers	Hot and sweet peppers
Potatoes	Just other potatoes
Radish	Wild radish
Spinach	Only other spinach varieties
Squash	Cucurbita maxima, pepo, and moschata species will all cross.
Tomato	Self-fertilizing. Some will cross under rare circumstances.
Turnip	Wild turnip
Watermelon	Citrons

Seed Viability

Years	Plants
1	Parsnips, garlic cloves (6-8 months)
2	Onions, chives
3	Beans, carrots, chervil, coriander, corn, leeks, lettuce, peas, parsley, peppers, tomatillos
4	Broccoli, cabbage, cauliflower, collards, fennel, kale, pumpkin, chard, tomatoes (up to 10 in optimal conditions), quinoa
5	Amaranth, asparagus, basil, Brussels sprouts, Chinese cabbage, celeriac, cucumbers (up to 10 in optimal conditions), dill, endive, kohlrabi, muskmelons, radish, spinach, turnip, watercress
6	Beets, orach, squash, watermelon
7	Artichoke, celery, eggplant, sunflower
8	Endive

Two things to keep in mind

Seed Saving: I have found saving seeds drastically impacts companion planting. When a plant goes to seed it grows taller and wider, changes soil chemistry and nutrient availability, falls down on other plants, and shifts the aesthetics.

Timing and Arranging: when planning your companion garden consider the space a plant needs, how high it grows, what soil conditions it prefers, how much water and light it needs, and how long it takes before harvest. An example would be planting cucumbers with corn. If you plant cucumbers and corn at the same time the corn will be overtaken and sometimes negatively impacted. By planting corn first and allowing it to reach a few feet before the cucumbers will insure a mutual relationship between the plants. Refer to the reference tables starting on page 67 for statistical data. Search online for plant pictures to gain a visual understanding of how much space a plant takes up.

Happy Gardening!

REFERENCES

Alway, Sara. *Soil Mates: Companion Planting for Your Vegetable Garden*. Quirk, 2011.

Bradley, Fern Marshall., et al. *The Organic Gardener's Handbook of Natural Pest and Disease Control: a Complete Guide to Maintaining a Healthy Garden and Yard the Earth-Friendly Way*. Rodale, 2010.

Cranshaw, Whitney, and David J. Shetlar. *Garden Insects of North America: the Ultimate Guide to Backyard Bugs*. Princeton University Press, 2018.

Cunningham, Sally Jean. *Great Garden Companions: a Companion Planting System for a Beautiful, Chemical-Free Vegetable Garden*. Rodale Press, 2000.

Druse, Kenneth, and Ellen Hoverkamp. *Natural Companions: the Garden Lover's Guide to Plant Combinations*. Stewart, Tabori & Chang, 2012.

"Entomology and Nematology Department." *UF/IFAS - University of Florida, Institute of Food and Agricultural Sciences*, entnemdept.ufl.edu/.

Greer, Allison, and Timothy Greer. *Companion Planting for the Kitchen Gardener: Tips, Advice, and Garden Plans for a Healthy Organic Garden*. Skyhorse Publishing, 2014.

Jeffery, Josie. *The Mix and Match Guide to Companion Planting: an Easy, Organic Way to Deter Pests, Prevent Disease, Improve*

Flavor, and Increase Yields in Your Vegetable Garden. Ten Speed Press, 2014.

Kress, Stephen W. *The Audubon Society Guide to Attracting Birds: Creating Natural Habitats for Properties Large and Small*. Comstock Publishing Associates, 2006.

"Los Angeles County Programs." *Los Angeles County*, celosangeles.ucanr.edu/files/121762.pdf .

Mayer, Dale. *The Complete Guide to Companion Planting: Everything You Need to Know to Make Your Garden Successful*. Atlantic Publishing Group, Inc., 2015.

McClure, Susan. *Rodale's Successful Organic Gardening: Companion Planting*. Rodale Press, 1994.

"Mushroom-Based Natural Insecticide." *Green*, green-mom.com/mushroom-based-natural-insecticide/#.XTO0UetKjIU.

Riotte, Louise. *Carrots Love Tomatoes: Secrets to Companion Planting for Successful Gardening*. Storey Publishing, 1998.

Riotte, Louise. *Roses Love Garlic: Companion Planting and Other Secrets of Flowers*. Storey Books, 1998.

Rodale, Maria. *Maria Rodale's Organic Gardening: Your Seasonal Companion to Creating a Beautiful and Delicious Garden*. Rodale Press, 1998.

Sewak, David, and Kristin Sewak. *Mycelial Mayhem: Growing Mushrooms for Fun, Profit and Companion Planting*. New Society Publishers, 2016.

Titchmarsh, Alan. *The Gardener's Year: Ultimate Month-by-Month Gardening Handbook*. BBC Books, 2006.

"UC Statewide IPM Program." *Home Page - UC Statewide IPM Program*, ipm.ucanr.edu/.

Willis, R. J. *The History of Allelopathy*. Springer, 2008.

Ziegler, Lisa. *Vegetables Love Flowers: Companion Planting for Beauty and Bounty*. Cool Springs Press, 2018.

Corn, clovers, & pumpkin

ABOUT THE AUTHOR

Tobias lives in the Evergreen State with his wife and beautiful children. He spends his time playing in the garden, connecting with nature, and enjoying his time with friends and family. To learn more about the author check out his traveling memoire, *A Different Road: From Bum to Mystic*

CPSIA information can be obtained
at www.ICGtesting.com
Printed in the USA
FSHW010959080520
70063FS